DEVOTION TO ❧ ❧ ❧ ❧
ST. ANTHONY OF PADUA
THE NOVENA OF NINE TUESDAYS
AND PRAYERS IN HIS HONOR ❧ ❧

. COMPILED FROM APPROVED SOURCES BY .

REV. BONAVENTURE HAMMER, O. F. M.

CINCINNATI:

YOUNG MEN'S SODALITY OF ST. FRANCIS CHURCH,

1889.

EDITION OF 1908.

Preface.

THE following pages were originally written in German, and published by the Sodality of the Blessed Virgin Mary, established under the care of the Franciscan Fathers at St. Francis Church, Cincinnati, Ohio. Having received the approbation of His Grace, the MOST REV. W. H. ELDER, Archbishop of Cincinnati, and of the VERY REV. JEROME KILGENSTEIN, O.F.M., Provincial of the Franciscan Province of Cincinnati, the pamphlet gained many friends: three editions were printed within less than a year, and numerous applications for an English version were made.

To satisfy this latter demand this edition was prepared, in the hope that it will contribute towards the spread of a devotion so fruitful of extraordinary results—the devotion to St. Anthony of Padua.

CINCINNATI, O., May 1, 1889.

St. Anthony of Padua.

St. Anthony of Padua was born in the year 1195, in Lisbon, Portugal. His parents were virtuous, wealthy and of noble birth. Ferdinand was the name given to the Saint in baptism, which was changed to Anthony when he became a Franciscan. His father wished him to choose the profession of arms, but Ferdinand had no military ambition, and loved nothing better than prayer, study and retirement. He began the higher course of studies under the Canons of St. Augustine, devoting himself to the study of rhetoric, philosophy, and theology with great enthusiasm and wonderful success in the Monastery of the Holy Cross near Coimbra. In the year 1220 the mangled bodies of three martyred Franciscans, victims of the fierce fanaticism of the Moors, were brought to Coimbra. Ferdinand felt an ardent longing spring up

5

in his heart to become a Franciscan, and, if God willed it, meet a death similar to theirs. He applied for admission to the Order of St. Francis, and was received into the Franciscan Monastery of St. Anthony, near Coimbra. At his own request, he was appointed assistant in the African Missions, but scarcely had he landed on the coast of Africa, when he was laid down by a local intermittent fever, which wasted his strength and confined him to a sick bed, till the tide of life seemed slowly ebbing away. He was obliged to return to his native country, and was brought on board of a ship about to sail for Portugal, but contrary winds sprang up and forced it to put by at Messina, in Sicily. The fresh sea breezes had expelled the fever from his system and left him convalescent, but without strength. He disembarked with the others.

When on shore, Anthony learned that St. Francis was then holding a chapter of the Order at Assisi, and the wish to see the Holy Founder determined him to go

thither. He journeyed toward Assisi, saw
and conversed with St. Francis, and obtained permission to remain in Italy.
Carefully concealing his intellectual gifts
and scholarly education, he applied in vain
to several Superiors to attach him to their
communities, until at last the Guardian of
St. Paul's Monastery near Bologna consent-
ed to receive him, and appointed him to
assist in the kitchen. His abilities and
great learning would have remained hidden
forever, had not Providence directed other-
wise. When he had been nearly two years
in the kitchen some members of the monastery, including Anthony, were sent to Forli,
and for a few days occupied the same
Monastery with the Dominicans. One
night, after supper, it was suggested that
some one of their number should preach.
All declined, on the ground of want of pre-
paration. Last of all, Anthony was asked,
but he also promptly declined. To his
utter astonishment, his Superior command-
ed him under obedience to preach as best
he could. The text of Scripture was as-

signed to him, and he rose to speak. The
first few sentences were spoken slowly,
spoken as if he were gradually collecting
his thoughts, or hesitating to tear off the
mask that had hitherto concealed his learning. Then his voice rose clear, firm, and
gracefully modulated, till he seemed no
longer the same man. Quotations most
happily chosen from all parts of the Scripture and from the Fathers of the Church
succeeded, like an army in close array, one
upon another. His hearers sat surprised,
spellbound; they had all heard other orators,
but never any to compare with him; they
felt his superiority, and that they were
mere disciples listening to the voice of a
master.

St. Francis heard with delight of this
great treasure hidden and discovered within
his Order. He wrote to him, appointing
him to teach theology, and had him
ordained priest. He taught theology with
great success, but gradually he abandoned
the lecture-room to devote himself more
exclusively to the conversion of sinners,

making his home principally at Padua. When St. Anthony first went to the latter place, there was no Franciscan Convent in the city, and the nearest was in Arcella, over a mile from Padua. It was extremely inconvenient for Anthony to go to Arcella every day, as his labors, both in the pulpit and in the confessional, were often protracted to a late hour in the night. With the permission of his Superior, he took up his abode, on such occasions, at the house of Count Tisco, a man of great piety and devoted to our Saint. The Count set apart a room in the house for Anthony, a secluded room, such as Anthony loved, where he would be least likely to be disturbed by visitors. One day, when the Count happened to be near the room, he was surprised to see the streams of light issuing from it, and looking in, he beheld Anthony with a little child in his arms, whom he lovingly caressed. Rays of divine light surrounded the head of the lovely child, and while the Count was still gazing full of awe and wonder, the vision disappeared. Anthony, recognizing he had been observed, begged the Count not to mention to anyone what he had seen, and the latter faithfully kept the secret during the Saint's life, but considered himself at liberty to reveal it after Anthony's death. This is the incident referred to in all the Saint's pictures.

The fruits of St. Anthony's missionary labors were wonderful. He preached usually in large cathedrals or in the open fields, because the mere intimation that he was about to preach drew thousands to the place. In the villages which he entered on his round of apostolic labor, all work was suspended for the day. The tradesman would lay aside his tools, with his task unfinished; the farmer would unyoke his oxen, with his field half ploughed; the aged and the young, rich and poor, would leave business or pleasure to listen with wonder and delight to this poor Franciscan, whom nature had made an orator and the grace of God a saint. Wherever he went, old feuds were healed, scandals suppressed or fearlessly rebuked, justice and mercy taught

towards the poor, till even usurers were
seen to relax their grasp on their ill-gotten
wealth and make restitution of their dis-
honest gains. God, at the same time,
wrought many miracles through the Saint.
He everywhere healed the sick, gave sight
to the blind, and hearing and speech to the
deaf and the dumb.

St. Anthony, when in Rome, preached
before the Pope and the Sacred College,
and with such effect, that His Holiness,
speaking of him afterwards to the Cardinals,
called him the "ARK OF THE COVENANT,"
meaning thereby, that his mind was a store-
house of sacred learning and profound
knowledge of the Scriptures.

Leaving Rome, St. Anthony retired to
Mt. Alverno—the wild, precipitous moun-
tain where St. Francis had received the
sacred stigmata. There he passed from
two to three months, the happiest of his
life, and it was with feelings of deep re-
gret that he left its peace and solitude to
preach the Lent in Padua. After Easter
he retired to Campo San Pietro, nine

miles from Padua, where there was a small Franciscan Convent. His health and strength had failed. His brethren thought it the result of overwork to be got rid of by rest, but he knew and said it was the advancing shadow of death. When the malady increased, he asked to be taken back to his convent in Padua. He was carried in a litter, and on hearing of his approach, the whole city went forth to meet him. Further progress was found impossible, and he was taken to a convent near by, within the suburbs of the city. Next morning he confessed and communicated, and, soon after, his face lit up and his eyes sparkled with delight. In answer to a question, he replied: "BRETHREN, I SEE THE LORD." After receiving Extreme Unction and joining in the recital of the seven penitential psalms, and his favorite hymn to the Blessed Virgin "O GLORIOSA DOMINA", he calmly expired on June 13, 1231. At the moment of his death hundreds of children went forth into the streets, of their own accord, and shouted aloud: "THE SAINT IS DEAD; ST. ANTHONY IS DEAD!"

After his death, so many miracles were wrought through the intercession of St. Anthony, that he was canonized the following year. Thirty-two years after his death, a stately church was erected under his invocation in Padua, and his remains were translated thither. St. Bonaventure, who was present on the occasion, tells us that, while the flesh of the body was all consumed, the tongue was incorrupt, fresh and ruddy as in life. Can we wonder that the tongue was preserved from corruption, whose eloquence had so often proclaimed the glory of God and saved thousands of souls from eternal ruin? The chapel containing the tomb is a marvel of its kind. Gorgeous splendor surrounds the grave of this poor son of St. Francis: this humble Saint who loved above all things to be hidden and unknown, but whom art, genius and religion delight to honor—St. Anthony of Padua.

The Novena of Nine Tuesdays in Honor of St. Anthony.

St. Anthony's happy death occurred on Friday, and his burial was appointed for the following Tuesday. No miracles had been performed through the Saint's intercession until the latter day, when the sacred remains were taken to their last resting place. Tuesday was, therefore, from that time, naturally chosen as a day especially appropriate for devotion to St. Anthony, and that such choice was acceptable to God was confirmed by innumerable indications ever since. It was not, however, until nearly four hundred years after the death of the Saint that the peculiar Novena of nine successive Tuesdays was recommended by himself. The occasion was as follows: In the year 1617, at Bologna, a lady of rank besought St. Anthony with special fervor to obtain for her a particular

14

grace. She was made assured, by an unwonted sense of interior consolation, that her prayer had been heard, and in the following night she beheld the Saint in a dream, encircled with rays, and heard him say: "O WOMAN, FOR NINE TUESDAYS, ONE AFTER THE OTHER, MAKE VISITS TO THE CHURCH OF MY ORDER; ON EACH OF THOSE DAYS APPROACH THE HOLY SACRAMENTS OF PENANCE AND OF THE ALTAR; THEN PRAY BEFORE MY PICTURE, AND WHAT YOU ASK, YOU SHALL OBTAIN." The pious lady performed the Novena according to these directions, and obtained what she had so fervently implored.

The Novena of Nine Tuesdays, in honor of St. Anthony of Padua, was therefore immediately spread all over Catholic Europe. How pleasing to God and to St. Anthony the exercise of this devotion is, we learn from the countless miracles and graces which God has been pleased to vouchsafe through its means. From the innumerable examples of the fruit derived from this peculiar Novena, the following are mentioned as particularly striking and perfectly authenticated: A Lady of Turin was, through it, miraculously preserved from the effects, first of poison, then of violence. In Rome, 1649, a young lady's character and peace of mind were restored by a most remarkable intervention of the Saint, during the celebration of a sacred function. Moreover, the following cases of deliverance from mortal disease are related: One of a boy near Cologne, whose cure of a malignant swelling began on the first and was completed on the last Tuesday of the Novena; and of two others—the first, of a noble lady who was afflicted with a fatal interior infirmity; and the second, of a physician, who was dying of gangrene, both of whom were cured suddenly, in a moment, at the conclusion of the Novena.

The Seraphic Doctor, St. Bonaventure, declares that all miraculous graces may be obtained through the intercession of St. Anthony. This intercession is sought chiefly for the following objects: (1) For the restoration of things lost or stolen; (2)

for the recovery of health; (3) for a knowledge of the will of God relative to the choice of an occupation or vocation; (4) for the happy issue of our undertakings, whether in relation to our spiritual or temporal good. With regard to temporal blessings we should always pray with the condition that they be in accordance with the will of God, and conducive to the welfare of our souls. The essential requisite, moreover, is, that we always pray with a lively faith, a firm hope, and above all, with a heart free from mortal sin, then we may expect all graces and blessings from him, who during his mortal life, thought only of comforting and assisting the unhappy and afflicted.

The Novena of Nine Tuesdays is performed in the following manner:

(1) Visit, for nine consecutive Tuesdays, a church, if possible one served by Franciscans, hear Mass, and recite appropriate prayers.

(2) If allowed, and when possible, receive, on each of the Tuesdays, the holy

Sacraments of Penance and of the Altar, with due devotion.

(3) Strive, with all earnestness, to imitate the virtues of St. Anthony, especially his purity and humility.

(4) The exercises may be performed privately at home, before a picture of the Saint, if the church can not be visited.

Pious Practices for the Nine Weeks of the Novena.

TRUE devotion to the saints consists in the imitation of their virtues: we there-fore subjoin for every week of the Novena some pious practice, which is to be performed in addition to the prayers, in order to obtain the protection and intercession of St. Anthony the more readily.

FIRST WEEK.

Practice charity. For example: Be friendly towards those against whom you feel aversion. "If, therefore, thou offer thy gift at the altar, and there shalt remember that thy brother has anything against thee: leave there thy offering before the altar, and go first and be reconciled to thy brother; and then come and offer thy gift." (Matth. 5, 23, 24.)

SECOND WEEK.

Accept every cross which God sends you in a spirit of penance, saying with St. Augustine:

"O Lord, scorch, scathe and punish me in this world, do but spare me in the next." "If any man will follow me, let him deny himself, and take up his cross." (Mark 8, 34.)

THIRD WEEK.

Mortify your tongue. "If any man think himself to be religious, not bridling his tongue, but deceiving his own heart, this man's religion is in vain." (James 1, 26.)

FOURTH WEEK.

Strive to know and to amend your predominant fault. "The kingdom of God suffereth violence, and the violent bear it away." (Matth. 11, 12.)

FIFTH WEEK.

Offer up all good works during this week for the souls in Purgatory. "It is a holy and wholesome thought to pray for the dead, that they may be loosed from sins." (ii. Mach. 12, 46.)

SIXTH WEEK.

Remember, in everything you do, the presence of God. "Walk before me, and be perfect." (Gen. 17, 1.)

SEVENTH WEEK.

In the evening, on retiring, remember the hour of death, and say to yourself: Perhaps my awakening will be in eternity. Lord have mercy on me a poor sinner. "In all thy works remember thy last end, and thou shalt never sin." (Eccl. 7, 40.)

EIGHTH WEEK.

Offer up the prayers and good works of this week for the Church, the Holy Father, the bishops and priests. "Pray for one another, that you may be saved." (James 5, 16.)

NINTH WEEK.

Practice some slight mortification of your appetite. If possible, contribute your mite towards some good and pious work. "Prayer is good with fasting and alms, more than to lay up treasures of gold." (Tobias 12, 8.)

Prayers to St. Anthony for the Novena of Nine Tuesdays.

O GLORIOUS St. Anthony, safe refuge of the afflicted and distressed, who, through a miraculous
revelation, hast directed all those who seek thy
aid to approach thy altar, with the promise, that
whoever visits it for nine consecutive Tuesdays,
and there piously invokes thee, will feel the power
of thy intercession: I, a poor sinner, encouraged
by this promise, come to thee today with a firm
hope, and I rejoice in the great honor which our
Holy Mother, the Church, has shown to thee in
placing thy image on her altars. I pour forth my
prayer to thee; I implore thy aid, thy protection,
thy counsel and thy blessing. Obtain for me, I
beseech thee, my request in this necessity [*name
it*], provided it be not opposed to the will of God,
and the welfare of my soul. Should such, however,
be the case, obtain for me such other graces, as
shall be conducive to my salvation. Through
Christ, our Lord. Amen.

Prayer to the Infant Jesus in the Arms of St. Anthony.

O Jesus, my Saviour! who didst vouchsafe to appear to St. Anthony in the form of an infant, I implore Thee, through the love Thou didst bear to this Saint when he dwelt on earth, and which Thou now bearest to him in heaven, graciously hear my prayer, and assist me in my necessities. Who livest and reignest, world without end. Amen.

PRAYER.

Almighty and Eternal God! who didst glorify Thy faithful confessor, Anthony, with the perpetual gift of working miracles, graciously grant that what we confidently seek through his merits we may surely receive through his intercession. Through Christ, our Lord. Amen.

The Responsory of St. Anthony of Padua.

Si quaeris miracula,
Mors, error, calamitas,
Daemon, lepra fugiunt,
Aegri surgunt sani.

Cedunt mare, vincula;
Membra, resque perditas
Petunt et accipiunt
Juvenes et cani.

Pereunt pericula,
Cessat et necessitas;
Narrent hi, qui sentiunt,
Dicant Paduani.

Cedunt mare, vincula;
Membra, resque perditas
Petunt et accipiunt
Juvenes et cani.

Gloria Patri et Filio,
Et Spiritui Sancto.

Cedunt mare, vincula,
Membra, resque perditas
Petunt et accipiunt
Juvenes et cani.

V.   Ora pro nobis, B. Antoni:
R.   Ut digni efficiamur promissionibus Christi.

OREMUS.

Ecclesiam tuam, Deus, Beati Antoni, confessoris
tui, commemoratio votiva lætificet, ut spiritualibus
semper muniatur auxiliis, et gaudiis perfruatur
æternis. Per Christum Dominum nostrum. Amen.

(*Translation.*)

If miracles thou fain wouldst see:
Lo! error, death, calamity,
The leprous stain, the demon flies,
From beds of pain the sick arise.

The hungry seas forego their prey,
The prisoner's cruel chains give way,
While palsied limbs, and chattels lost,
Both young and old recovered boast.

And perils perish; plenty's hoard
Is heaped on hunger's famished board.
Let those relate, who know it well,
Let Padua of her Patron tell.

The hungry seas forego their prey,
The prisoner's cruel chains give way,
While palsied limbs, and chattels lost,
Both young and old recovered boast.

May glory to the Father be,
And to the Son eternally,
And to the Spirit, in essence one,
In Persons three, be honor done.

The hungry seas forego their prey,
The prisoner's cruel chains give way,
While palsied limbs, and chattels lost,
Both young and old recovered boast.

V. Pray for us, Blessed Anthony:

R. That we may be made worthy of the promises of Christ.

LET US PRAY:

O God! let the votive commemoration of Blessed Anthony, Thy confessor, be a source of joy to Thy Church, that she may always be fortified with spiritual assistance and may deserve to possess eternal joy. Through Christ, our Lord. Amen.

His Holiness, Pope Pius IX., by a decree of the Sacred Congregation of Indulgence, January 25, 1866, granted to all the faithful, as often as they shall, with at least contrite heart and devotion, say this Responsory, with the versicle and prayer annexed, AN INDULGENCE OF ONE HUNDRED DAYS, and A PLENARY INDULGENCE, once a month, on any day, to all those who shall have said it for a month, provided that, being truly penitent, after Confession and Communion, they shall visit a church or public oratory, and there pray, for some time, for the intention of His Holiness.

Closing Prayer at the End of the Novena.

O Blessed St. Anthony, my faithful intercessor, I have now, through the grace of God and thy assistance, finished the pious exercises in thy honor. I had, indeed, the will and desire to do all in my power for thy greater honor and glory, but thou knowest my weakness and misery and want of devotion; wherefore, I beseech thee to make amends for all my failings, and to offer thy merits and good works for me, that I may find grace and hearing with God. Obtain for me, through thy merits, the blessing of a virtuous life, a true knowledge of my God and of myself, a perfect mortification of my senses, and a complete triumph over all temptations. I place myself under thy special protection, assist me to follow thy example in life and come to my aid in death: in that dread moment let me experience the might of thy help. Amen.

The Chaplet of St. Anthony.

The Chaplet of St. Anthony is composed of thirteen decades of three beads each. On the first bead of each decade is said the "Our Father;" on the second, the "Hail Mary," and on the third, "Glory be to the Father," etc. At the end the Responsory (see page 24) is recited.

Litany of St. Anthony.

(For Private Devotion.)

Lord have mercy on us!
Christ have mercy on us!
Christ hear us!
Christ graciously hear us!
Holy Mary,
Holy Father Francis,
St. Anthony of Padua,
Glory of the Order of Friars Minor,
Martyr in desiring to die for Christ,
Pillar of the Church,
Worthy priest of God,
Apostolic preacher,
Teacher of truth,
Conqueror of heretics,
Terror of evil spirits,
Comforter of the afflicted,
Helper in necessities,
Deliverer of captives,
Guide of the erring,
Restorer of lost things,
Chosen intercessor,
Continuous worker of miracles,

Pray for us!

Be merciful unto us, *Spare us, O Lord!*
Be merciful unto us, *Hear us, O Lord!*
From all evil,
From all sin, } *O Lord, deliver us!*

From all dangers of body and soul,
From the snares of the devil,
From pestilence, famine and war,
From eternal death,
Through the merits of St. Anthony,
Through his zeal for the conversion of sinners,
Through his desire for the crown of martyrdom,
Through his fatigues and labors,
Through his preaching and teaching,
Through his penitential tears,
Through his patience and humility,
Through his glorious death,
Through the number of his prodigies,
In the day of judgment,
We sinners,
That Thou vouchsafe to bring us to true
   penance,
That Thou vouchsafe to grant us patience in
   our trials,
That Thou vouchsafe to assist us in our neces-
   sities,
That Thou vouchsafe to hear our prayers and
   petitions,
That Thou vouchsafe to kindle the fire of divine
   love within us,
That Thou vouchsafe us the protection and
   intercession of St. Anthony,
Son of God,

O Lord, deliver us!

We beseech Thee, hear us!

Lamb of God, who takest away the sins of the
world, *Spare us, O Lord!*

Lamb of God, who takest away the sins of the world, *Graciously hear us, O Lord!*

Lamb of God, who takest away the sins of the world, *Have mercy on us, O Lord!*

Christ hear us!

Christ graciously hear us!

V. Pray for us, O Blessed St. Anthony!

R. That we may be made worthy of the promises of Christ!

LET US PRAY:

Almighty and eternal God! who didst glorify Thy faithful confessor, Anthony, with the perpetual gift of working miracles, graciously grant that what we confidently seek through his merits we may surely receive through his intercession. Through Christ, our Lord. Amen.

O Lord! may Thy holy confessor, Anthony, intercede for us, upon whom, adorned with heroic virtues, Thou didst bestow the gift of miracles, even unto working prodigious signs and wonders. Through Christ, our Lord. Amen.

Prayer to St. Anthony.

We salute thee, St. Anthony, lily of purity, ornament and glory of Christianity! We salute thee, great Saint, cherub of wisdom and seraph of divine love! We rejoice at the favors our Lord has so liberally bestowed on thee. In humility and confidence we entreat thee to help us, for we know that God has given thee charity and pity as well as power. Oh! then, behold our distress, our anxiety, our fears concerning—[*here name your request*]. We ask thee by the love thou didst feel towards the amiable little Jesus when He covered thee with His caresses. Oh! tell Him now of our wants. One sigh from that breast He so honored will crown our success, will fill us with joy. Oh! remember how complete thy bliss was as thou didst hold Him to thy breast, didst press thy cheek to His, and didst listen to His angelic voice.

We salute thee in spirit, O glorious favorite of God, and bow our guilty heads before thee in humble reverence, while we raise our sad hearts full of hope towards heaven and thee, for He who so often put Himself in thy arms will now fill thy hands with all we ask of thee. Give us, then, what we desire, angel of love, and we will publish thy grandeur, thereby to honor and glorify Him who so blessed thee. Amen.

Prayer to St. Anthony for the Restoration of Things Lost or Stolen.

O Blessed St. Anthony! the grace of God has made thee a powerful advocate in all necessities and the patron for the restoration of things lost or stolen: to thee I turn today with child-like love and heartfelt confidence. Oh, how many thousands hast thou miraculously aided in the recovery of lost goods! Thou wast the counsellor of the erring,

the comforter of the afflicted, the healer of the
sick, the raiser of the dead, the deliverer of the
captive, the refuge of the afflicted: to thee do I
hasten, O Blessed St. Anthony! help me in my
present affliction. I recommend what I have lost
to thy care, in the secure hope that thou wilt restore
it to me if it be to the greater glory of God and
to the spiritual benefit of my soul, that I may
praise and thank thee, in time and eternity, for
thy glorious intercession in my behalf. Amen.

Anthem to St. Anthony.

O Proles Hispaniæ,
Pavor infidelium,
Nova lux Italiæ,
Nobile depositum
Urbis Paduanæ:
Fer, Antoni, gratiæ
Christi patrocinium;
Ne prolapsis veniæ
Tempus, breve creditum,
Defluat inane.

O Hispania's progeny,
Fear of all the faithless lost,
Light, new born of Italy,
Buried treasure, matchless boast
Of the Paduan City:
Anthony, with patron power,
Jesus' grace for us obtain,
Lest the briefly granted hour
To the fallen—flow in vain,
Time of heavenly pity.

Contents.